WHERE THE EAGLE SOARS

WHERE THE EAGLE SOARS

OVER BRITISH COLUMBIA'S ISLANDS

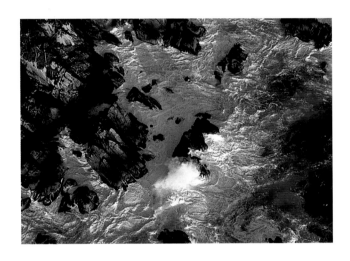

PHOTOGRAPHS BY RUSS HEINL

RAINCOAST BOOKS
Vancouver

BEAUTIFUL
BRITISH COLUMBIA
Magazine

This book, my first,

is dedicated to my first love, my wife,

Anne

whose unending love and absolute support

have given me the courage and vision to photograph

Where the Eagle Soars.

FIRST PUBLISHED IN CANADA IN 1994 BY

Raincoast Book Distribution Ltd.
112 East 3rd Avenue
Vancouver, BC V5T 1C8

Beautiful British Columbia
a Division of Great Pacific Industries Inc.
929 Ellery Street, Victoria, BC V9A 7B4

© Russ Heinl 1994
Foreword © Robert Bateman

Designed by Dean Allen
Printed and bound in Hong Kong through Mandarin Offset

CANADIAN CATALOGUING IN PUBLICATION DATA

Heinl, Russ, 1949-
  Where the eagle soars
ISBN 1-895714-46-X (bound). — ISBN 1-895714-44-3 (pbk.)

  1. Islands—British Columbia—Aerial photographs. 2. Islands—British Columbia—Pictorial works. 3. British Columbia—Aerial photographs. 4. British Columbia—Pictorial works. I. Beautiful British Columbia Magazine (Firm) II. Title.
FC3812.H44 1994   917.11'0022'2   C94-910181-8
F1087.8H44 1994

This book is printed on acid-free paper produced from selectively harvested trees. No clear-cut, rainforest or other endangered-species products were used. The manufacturing process also involves no dioxin-producing chlorine.

ALTHOUGH ART AND NATURE have been the most important things in my life, my university degree was in geography. In each of these areas, the work of Russ Heinl strikes a significant chord.

Heinl's photographic work definitely falls into the category of art. I remember having dinner one evening a few years ago with Lorraine Monk, former head of the National Film Board of Canada, Still Photography Division. I began talking about art and photography. She said, "What do you mean, art *and* photography?" I got the point. Many serious photographers are more visually creative than the average picture painter. The photographs in this book have been composed and crafted with the eye of an artist. Vermeer and Caravaggio used lighting to enhance the form and drama of their paintings. Heinl does the same thing in his choice of angle and position and time of day. In some pictures he uses dynamic shapes and rhythms in the same manner as the post-impressionists.

Nature, of course, is the main subject of his work. And the naturalist in me responded immediately to his portrayal of the variety of ecosystems we have in British Columbia. One of the key components of my philosophy is that variety is not only the "spice of life," it is what life is all about. We in B.C. are blessed with great variety in our natural areas. It is a treat to see these from a new perspective, and to linger over each photograph and imagine oneself rambling along the shore or through the forest. His pictures are so clear you can easily take a vicarious trip through the beauty spots of our province.

When I first began teaching high school geography in the 1950s, my best lessons were based on the analysis of oblique aerial photographs. Geographers are interested in exploring the reasons for inter-relationships in space. Why does that cliff become steep here and not there? Why does the river turn like this? How did human development occur in that particular way? Geography is like a detective story, with the answers laid out before us, if only we can read the clues. Every picture in Russ Heinl's *Where the Eagle Soars* gives us a wonderful display of this complex and beautiful world. I hope that appreciating this book will help us to appreciate and better protect our precious planet.

Robert Bateman, internationally renowned nature artist.

ROBERT BATEMAN

NO ONE HAS EVER ACCUSED ME of being a poet, but when I am called upon to express my thoughts about British Columbia, I wish I had the poet's gift. Having travelled the length and breadth of this beautiful province over a period of thirty-three years, in diverse capacities ranging from tourist and sport fisherman, through the various levels of a long career in the forestry industry and, ultimately, to Lieutenant-Governor, I feel uniquely privileged to have witnessed a fascinating cross-section of its economic, cultural and political development.

The big picture, however, and the picture which is so eloquently depicted in these pages, is the stunning physical beauty and natural wealth of the land. From aloft, it would appear that a benign Nature cradles us in her palm. In reality, the balance has tipped, and it is Nature which rests in our hands. Whether an environmental activist, logger, farmer, fisherman, politician or new immigrant, everyone who chooses to live here has a responsibility to work in harmony with each other and with nature to create a balance that is beneficial to all. Such a bountiful and magnificent landscape is truly deserving of our most stringent stewardship.

The Honourable Robert G. Rogers, former Lieutenant-Governor of British Columbia, Chancellor of the University of Victoria, OC, OBC, K.St.J., LL.D., D.Sc.M., CD

THE HON. ROBERT G. ROGERS

The machine silently awaits in the warm glow of pre-dawn.
Check and double check. There is no room for error.

At first light, the helicopter lifts free and vanishes
in a ghostly shroud of mist.

Below, the Pacific churns and boils, as pounding waves crash
onto the cathedral cliffs of de la Touche.

Steep canyon walls channel the howling winds.
Our machine shudders and groans in protest under their grasp.

Soaring high over the remote San Christoval Mountains,
ancient Haida totem poles at long last reveal themselves as never before.

This is the privileged domain of the "eagle," the aerial photographer.

BRITISH COLUMBIA'S ISLANDS are places of majesty and mystery, where the eagle soars over rugged natural beauty and an ever-changing tableau of ocean, rock, forest, and light. The Queen Charlotte Islands, Vancouver Island, and the Gulf Islands all cling to the continental shelf off Canada's west coast. Thanks to warm ocean currents, they share a mild climate and a tremendous wealth of plant and animal life. However, each place has its own unique ambience.

The Queen Charlotte Islands, known to the Haida people as *Haida Gwaii*, are part of Canada's westernmost land mass, and are separated from the mainland by Hecate Strait (the Inside Passage), a 96-kilometre (60-mile) stretch of sea. There are about 150 islands and islets in the group, with six main islands—Langara, Graham, Moresby, Lyell, Kunghit, and Louise—stretching for a total of 250 kilometres (156 miles). There are only 6,000 residents living and working on the edge of a vast wilderness of rainforest, jagged mountain peaks and enchanting fjords. Ancient, now abandoned, Haida villages show the roots of a still vibrant culture. Many residents and visitors have commented that the Queen Charlottes

A breathtaking view, shot from outside the helicopter, with Nanaimo in the distance.

seem saturated with their own history, as though the dense forests and ocean mists have embraced the spirits of the past.

About 230 kilometres (143 miles) to the south lies the huge land mass of Vancouver Island. From the magnificent snow-capped peaks of Strathcona Provincial Park, to rolling acres of cultivated fields and endless stretches of sandy beach, when viewed from above the island offers up a delightful mosaic of geographical variation. British Columbia's provincial capital, Victoria, spreads across the southernmost point of Vancouver Island, surrounded by water on three sides.

The Gulf Islands are the jewels of the West Coast. Nestled in sheltered waters between Vancouver Island and the mainland, they have a more pastoral feel than the Queen Charlottes or Vancouver Island although they are also prey to the occasional spectacular wind storm. For most of the year, though, their tranquil coves and many channels make the area a boater's paradise. The more populated islands—Saltspring, North and South Pender, Galiano, Gabriola, Mayne and Saturna—are linked with Vancouver Island and the mainland by government-operated ferries.

The spectacular islands of Canada's west coast were the inspiration for *Where the Eagle Soars*. I realised that aerial photography provided a unique opportunity to capture the islands as they have never been seen. As the project evolved, it became apparent that our journeys would require careful preparation and research. Over two years we consulted countless articles, maps, charts and archives, and interviewed many people about the history and geography of each area — searching for locations that would visually express the great variety and richness of the region.

Russ Heinl (in blue) preparing for a Snowbirds aerial shoot at CFB Comox.

Once each location had been confirmed, we began planning the photography sessions, taking into account that while the helicopter offers access to remote places, it also creates special challenges. Seasonal variations and often hostile weather imposed one kind of creative influence. I especially wanted to capture the ethereal light that follows a Pacific storm, which meant that we could not avoid coming face to face with some harsh conditions. The limitations of fuel capacity and flight distances presented yet another challenge. Each flight had to be carefully mapped out, in a grid of five-minute aerial segments, to ensure that our fuel supplies would allow us enough time to complete the assignment and return safely to our home base.

To bring the targeted areas into our sights we reached altitudes as high as 3,000 metres (10,000 feet) and dropped as low as 3 metres (10 feet). We always flew with my door removed, leaving me exposed to the extreme cold. Long sessions under these conditions, operating the heavy gyro-stabilized camera system, were exhausting. The pilot and I — after being slammed around by mountain turbulence and Pacific storms —

have spent hours thawing out and recomposing ourselves. But none of this mattered while we were in the air, viewing the incredible world beneath us.

As they work, some aerial photographers enter into a lucid state of mind, acutely focused only on what can be experienced through the camera's lens. While we were photographing, my only contact with the mechanical world of engines, fuel and turbulence was through the intercom that connected me to the pilot. During one session in the Queen Charlottes, my concentration was abruptly shattered. We had banked the helicopter steeply to my side, with the pilot crabbing the machine sideways as I stood braced on the outside cargo racks. I was completely engrossed in my work, composing an elongated shot over Hotspring Island, when there was a tremendous bang and a huge rush of air. The helicopter lurched downward, and I was thrown back into the cabin as the pilot quickly brought the helicopter under control. Only then did I realise that an extreme imbalance in cabin pressure had blown his door out; it was saved from falling only by the single wire-mesh restraining harness.

Flying in a single-engine aircraft into these remote areas, sometimes under foreboding weather conditions, became a test of personal resolve and dedication to my original vision. While there were many anxious moments, I also recall the exhilarating experiences that have made me feel so privileged. After one session in the Queen Charlottes, we were returning to home base when an intense rainbow suddenly appeared. As we flew the helicopter directly into the rainbow's arc, we became completely encircled by a multi-coloured halo of brilliant light. Aviators very aptly describe this phenomenon as "flying into the glory."   *Russ Heinl*

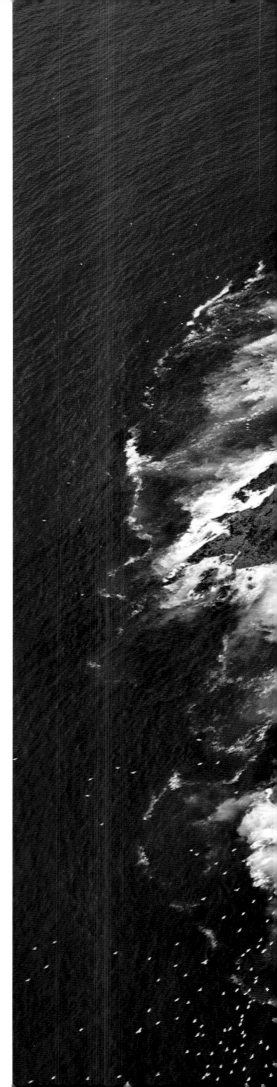

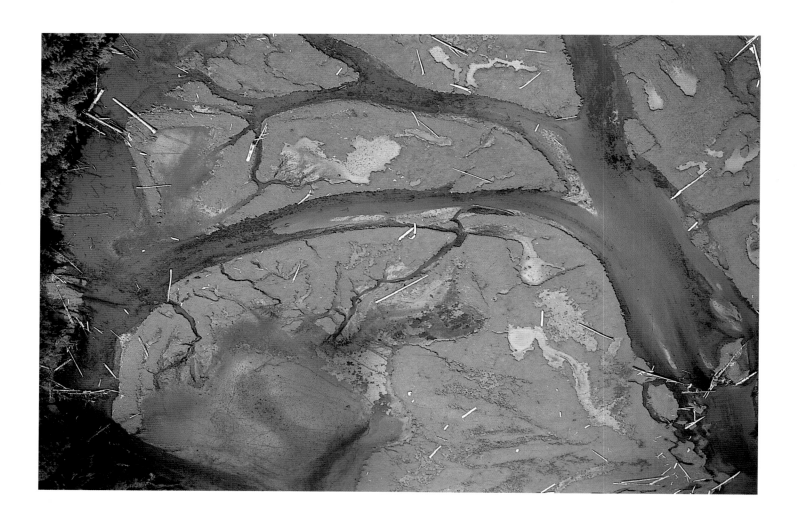

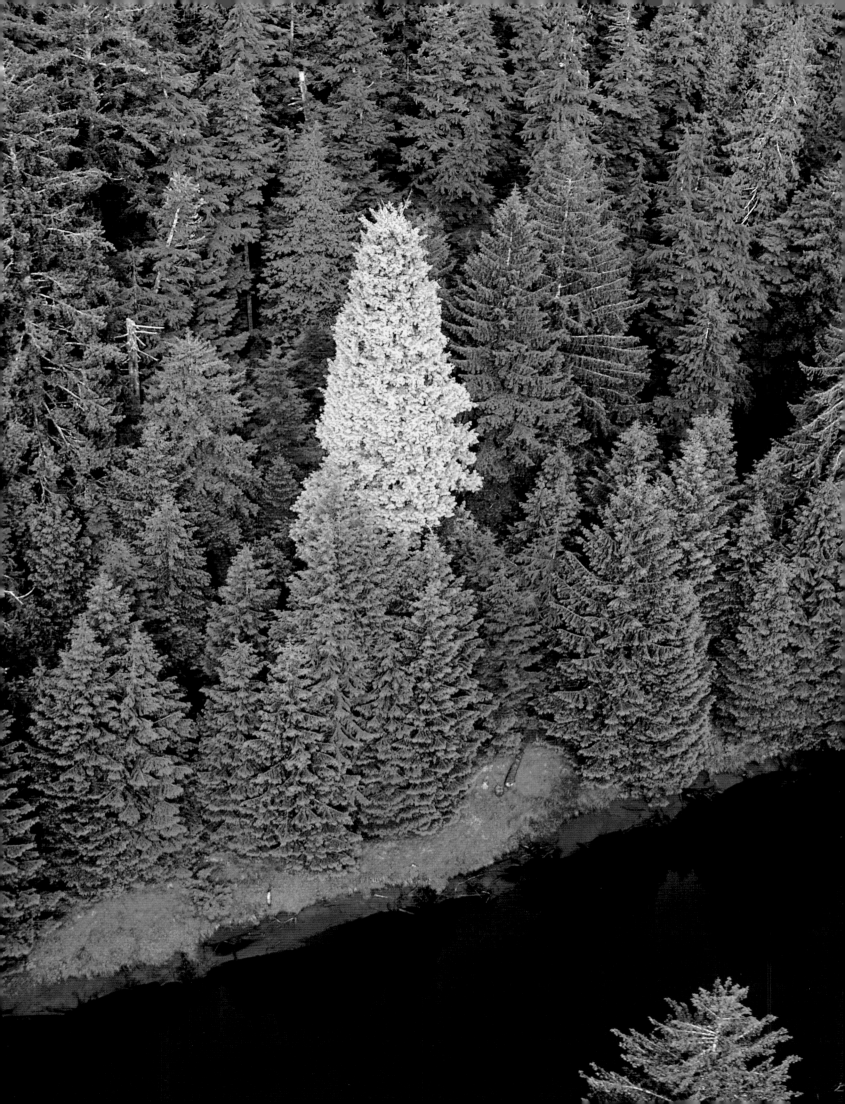

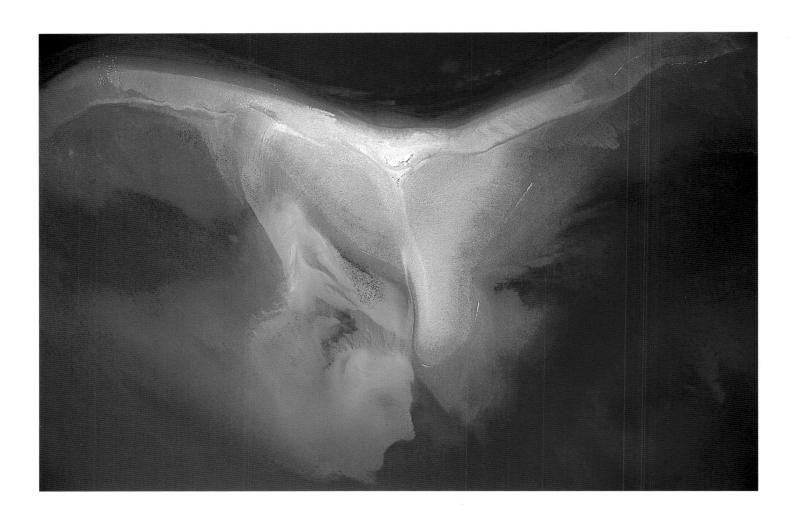

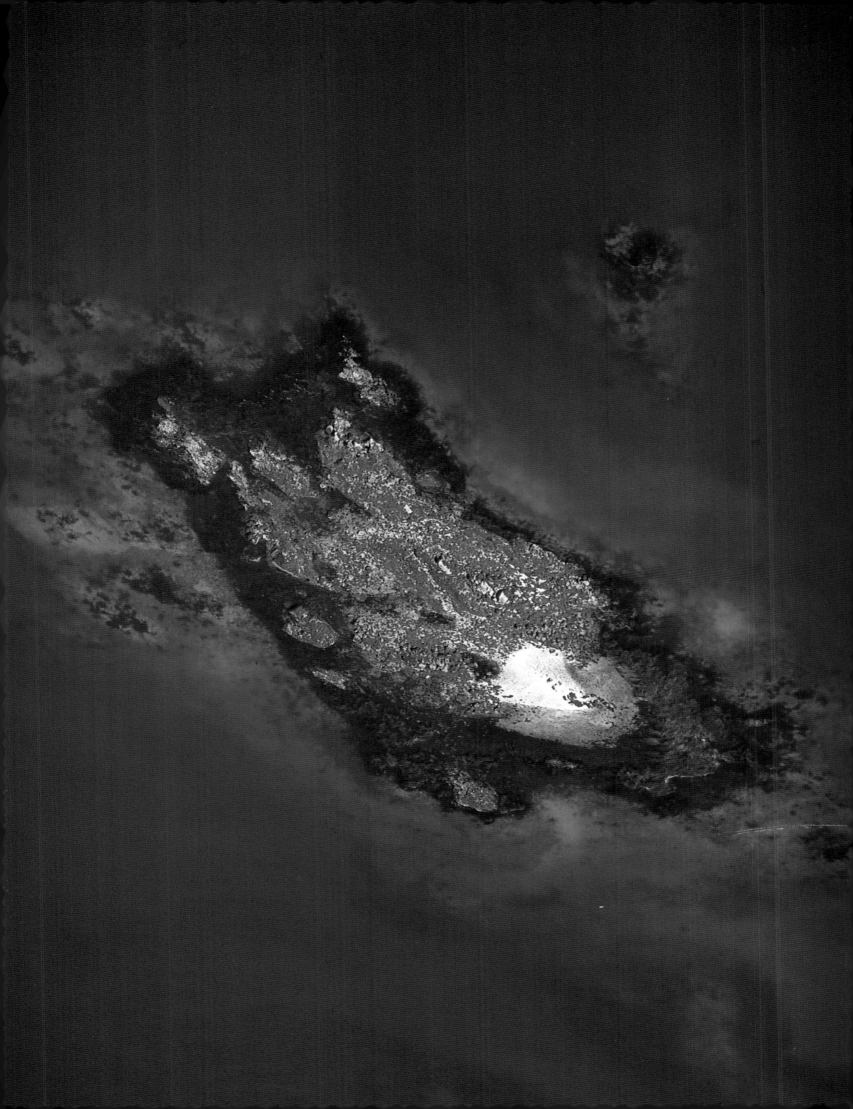

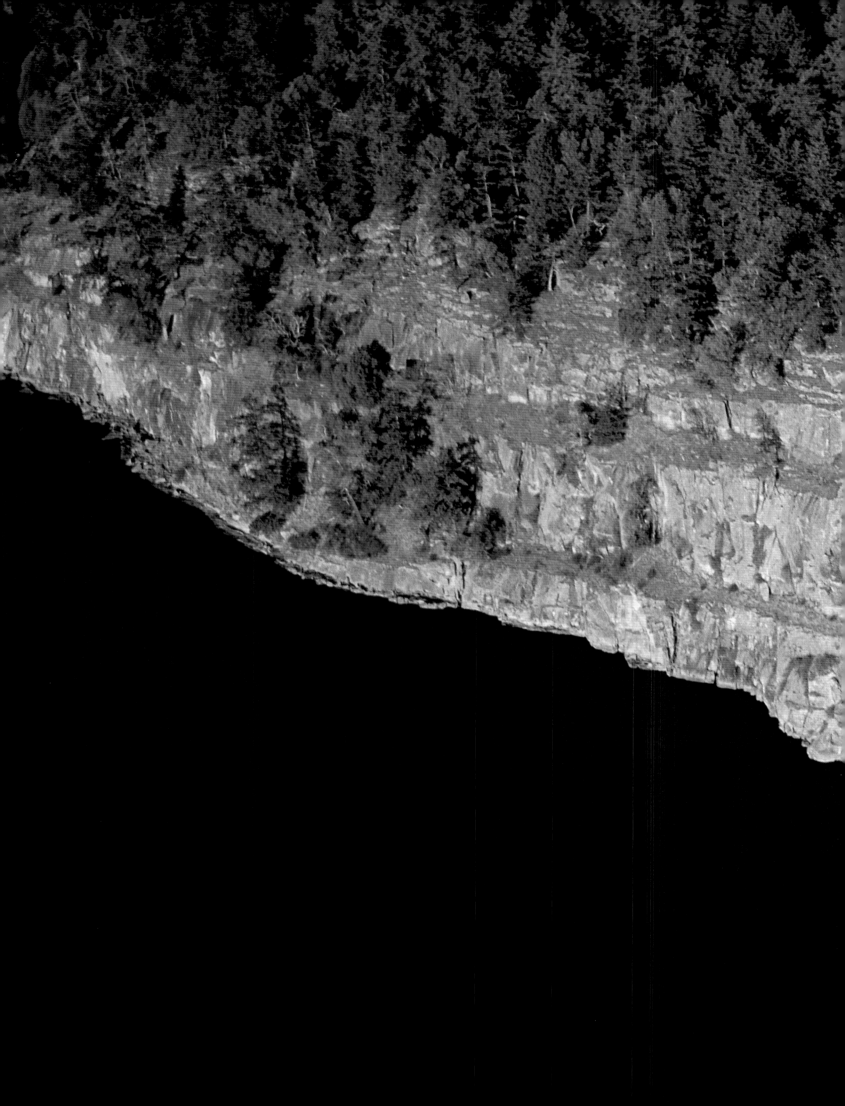

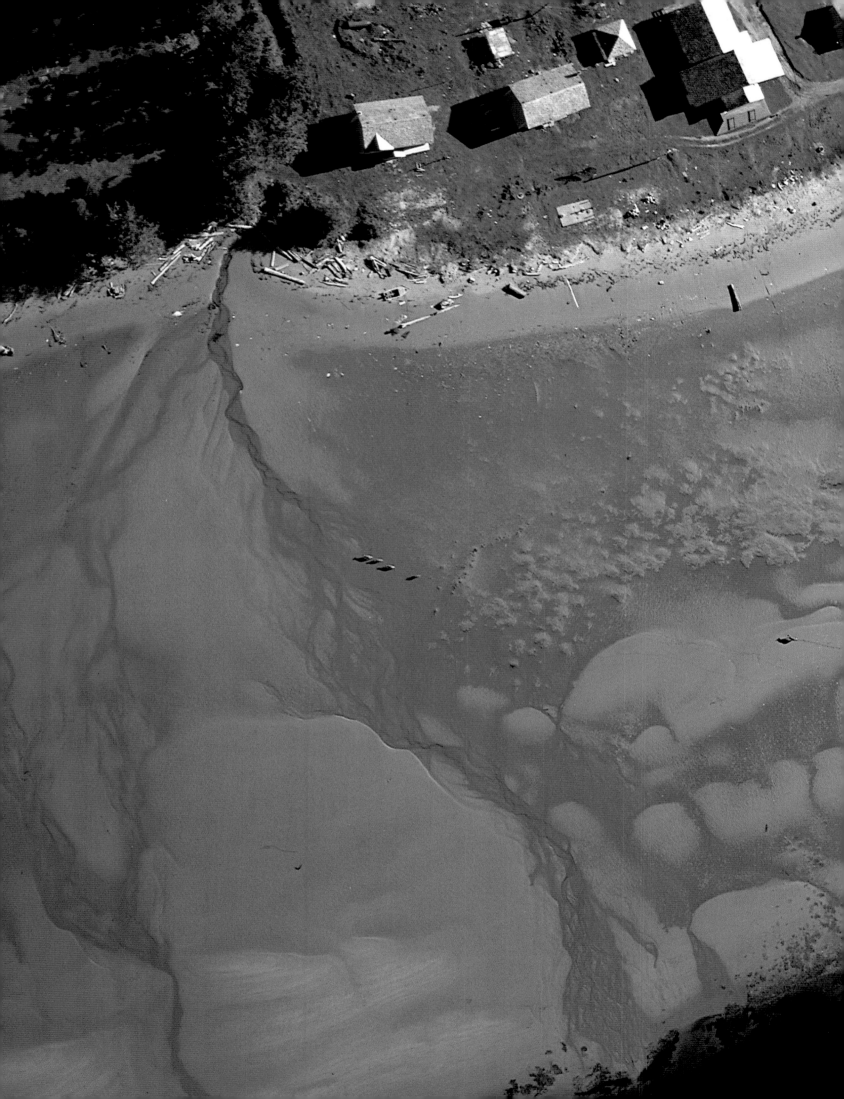

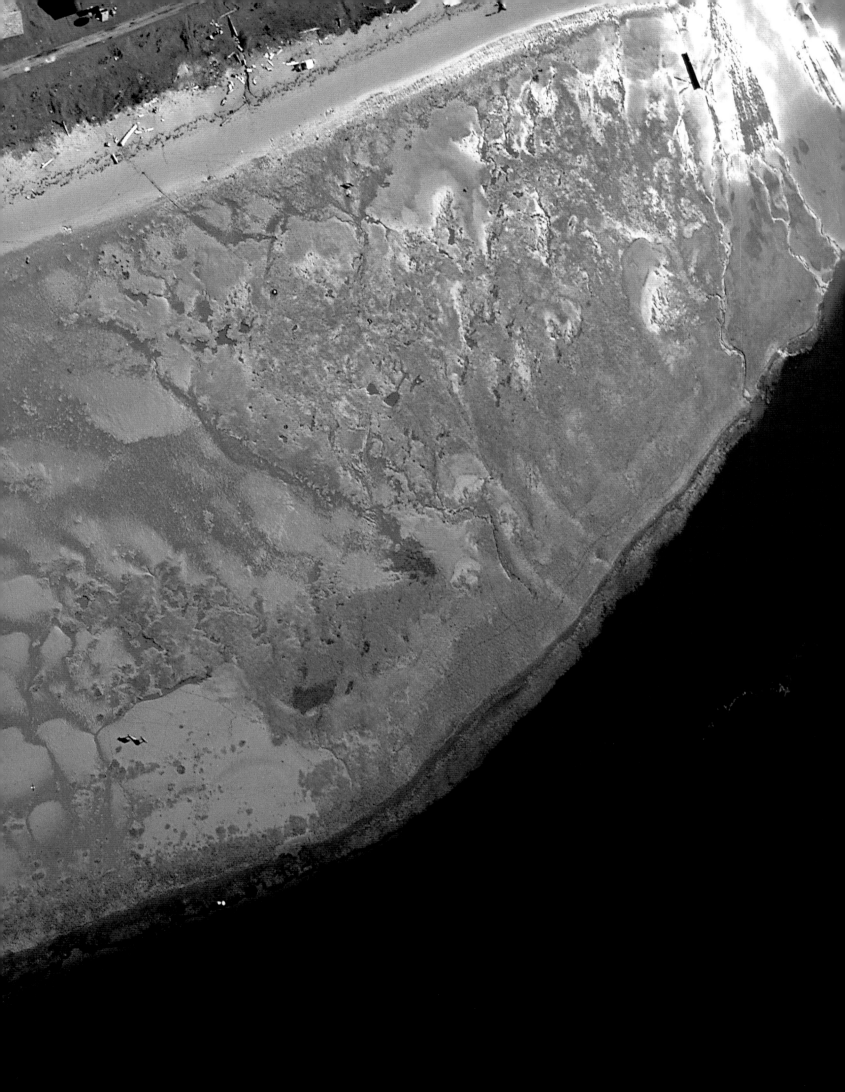

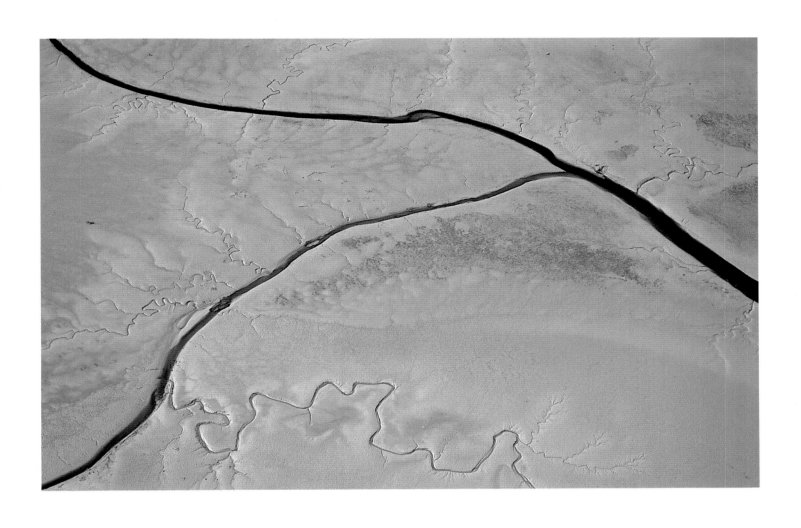

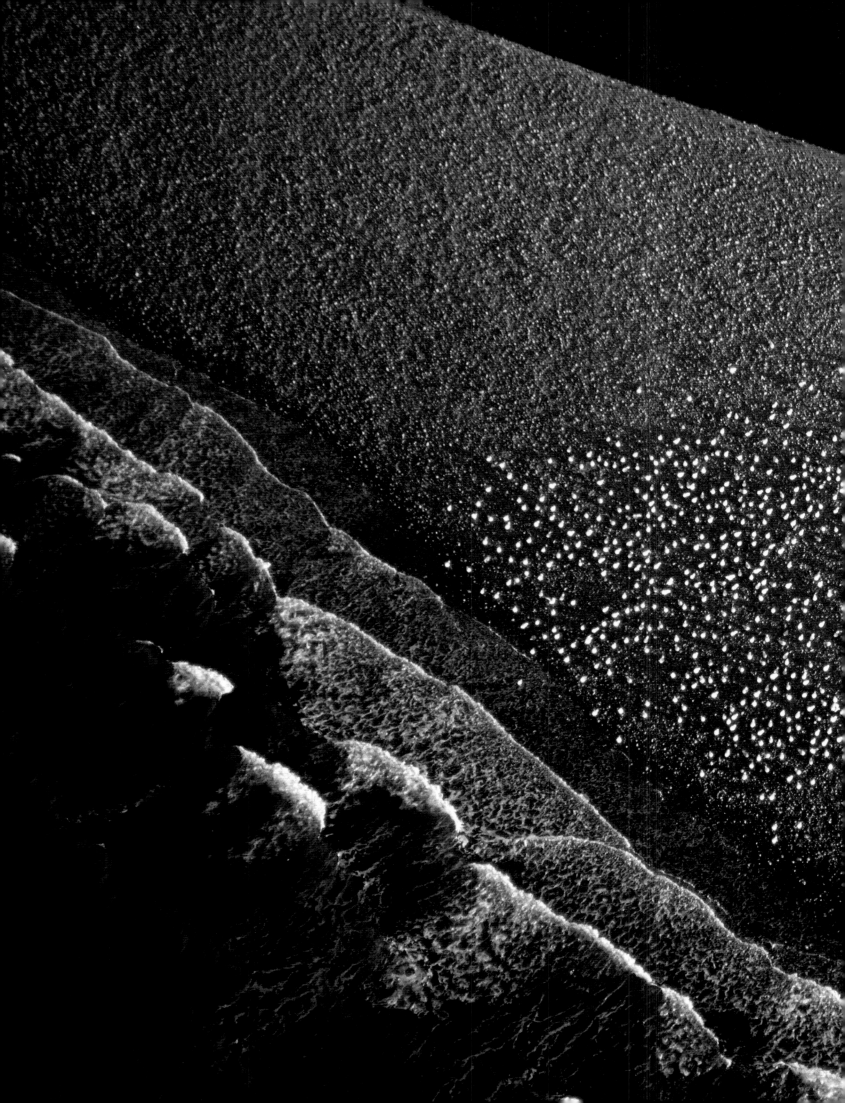

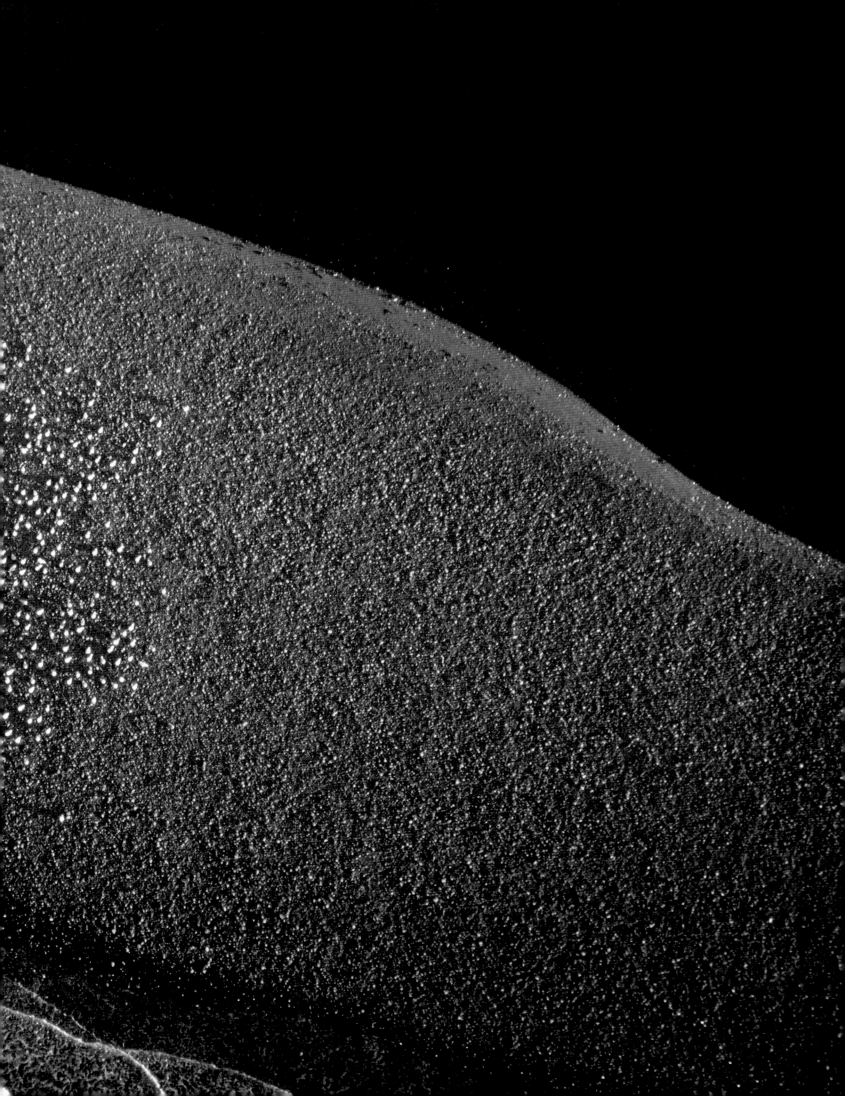

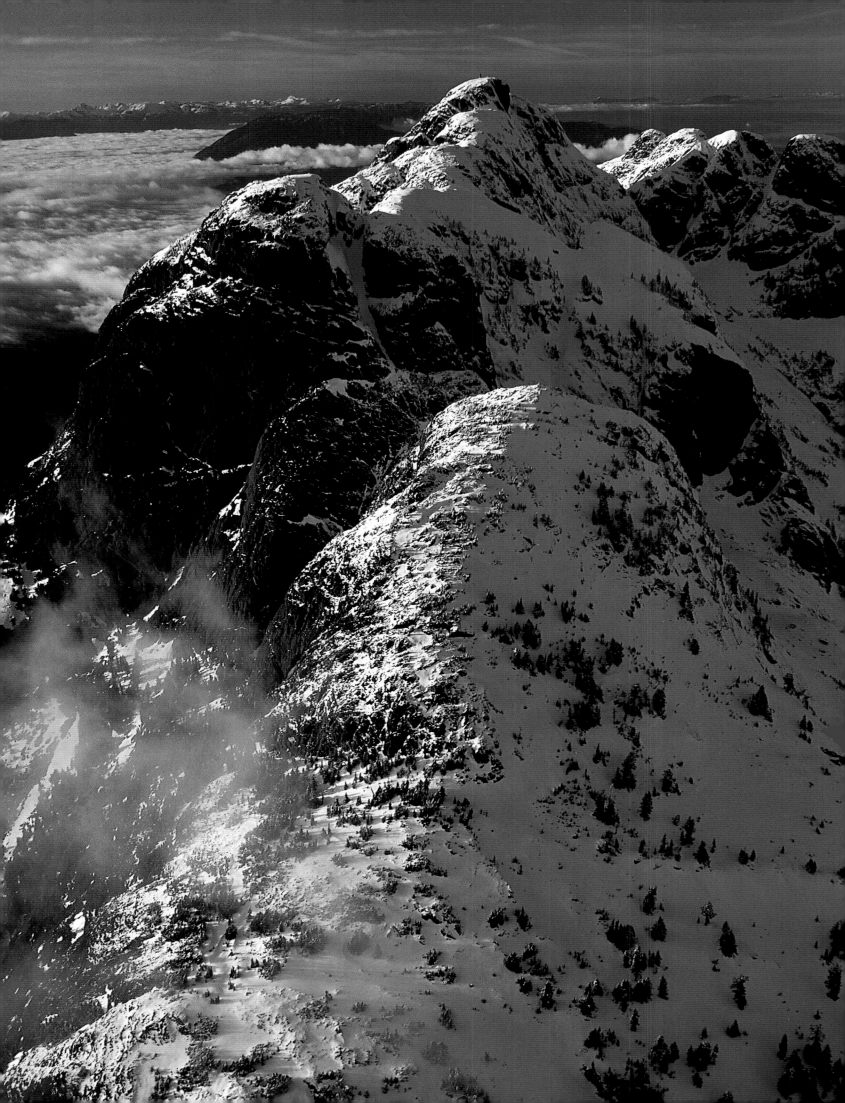

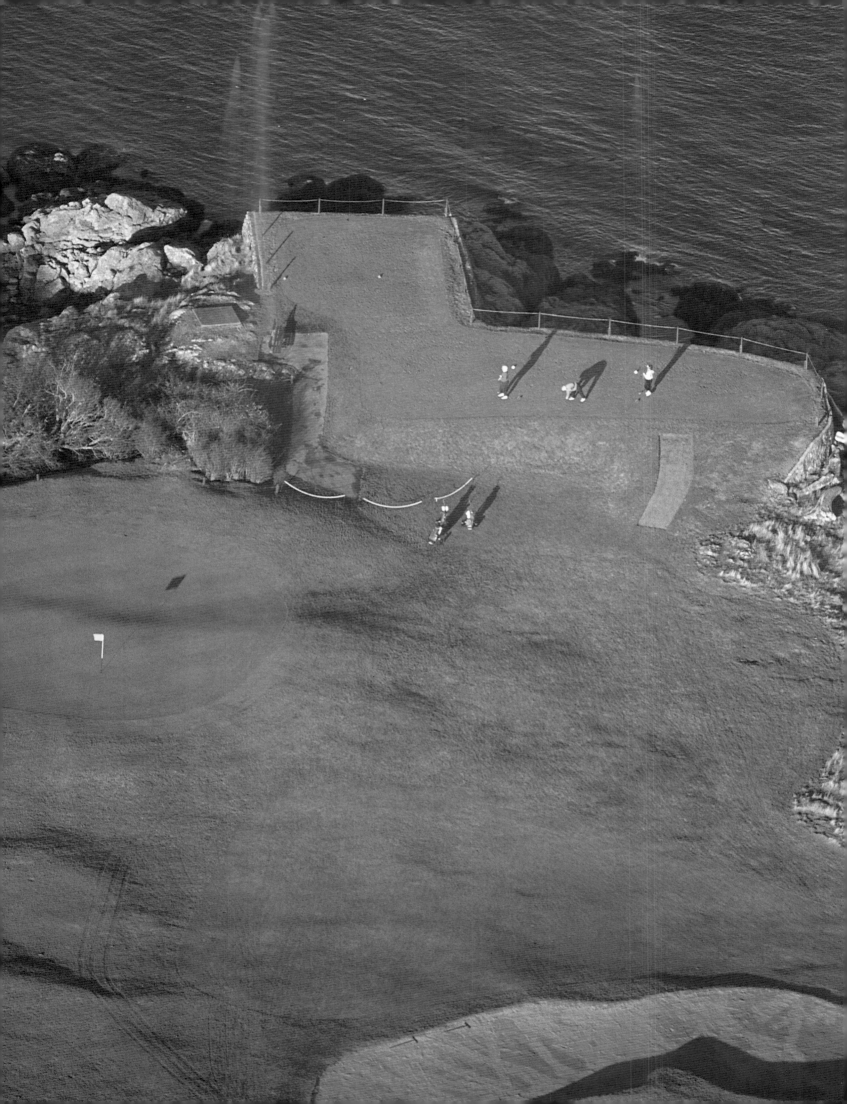

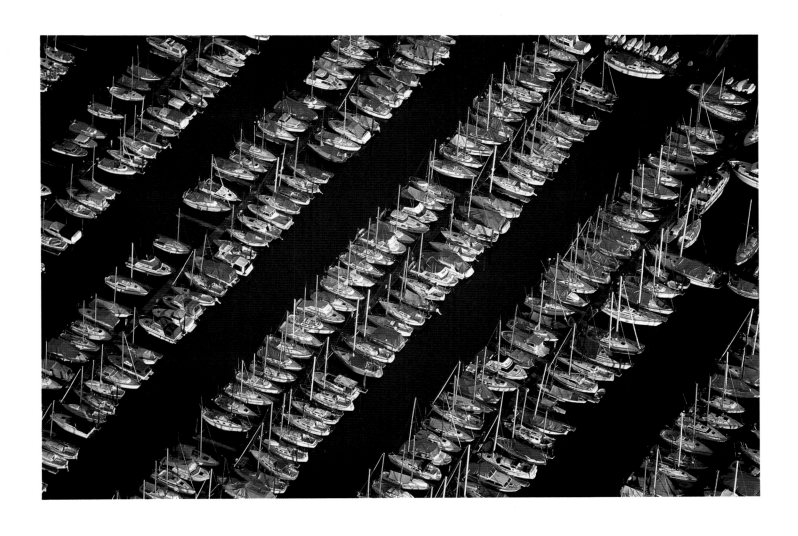

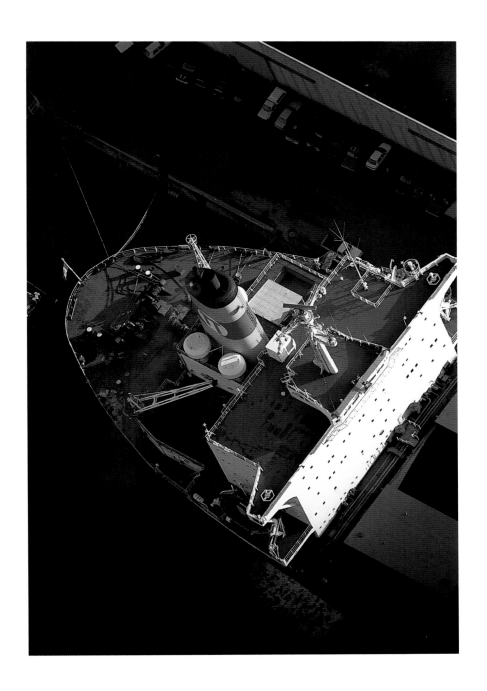

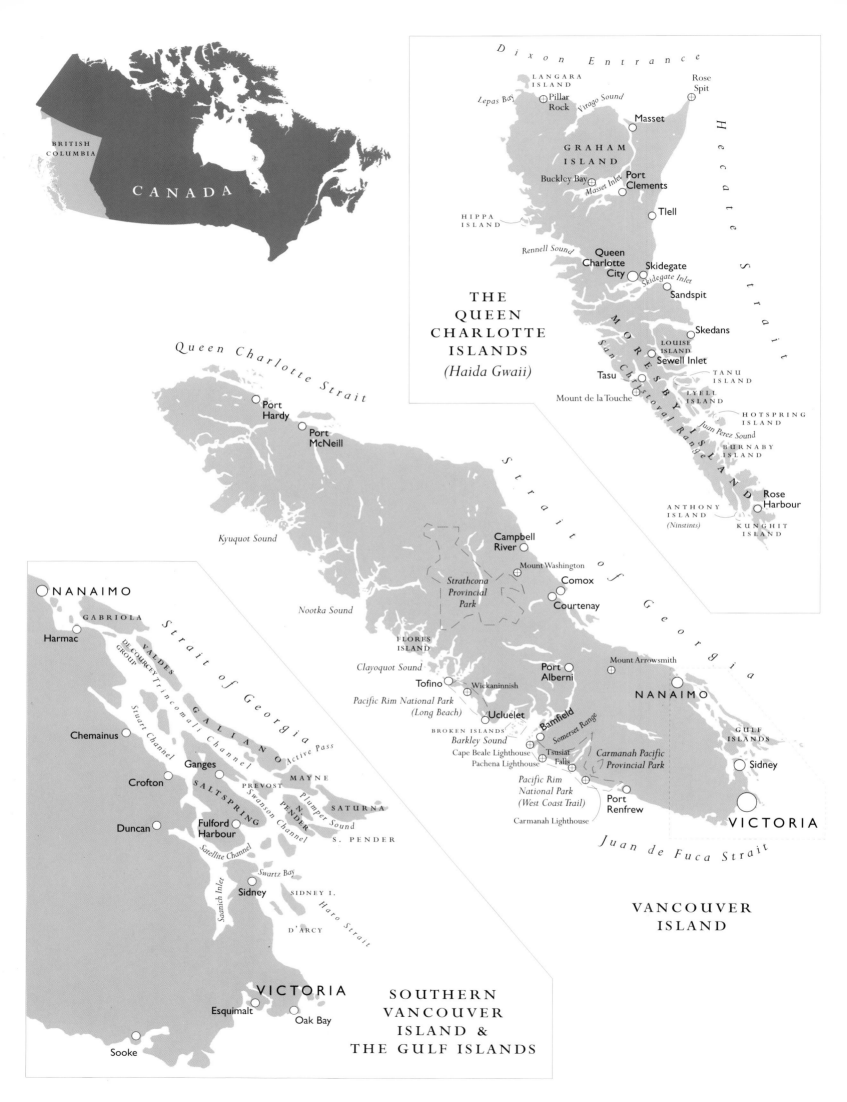

CANADA

BRITISH COLUMBIA

THE QUEEN CHARLOTTE ISLANDS *(Haida Gwaii)*

Dixon Entrance

LANGARA ISLAND
Lepas Bay
Pillar Rock
Virago Sound
Rose Spit
Masset
GRAHAM ISLAND
Buckley Bay
Masset Inlet
Port Clements
Tlell
HIPPA ISLAND
Rennell Sound
Queen Charlotte City
Skidegate
Skidegate Inlet
Sandspit
Skedans
LOUISE ISLAND
Sewell Inlet
TANU ISLAND
Tasu
LYELL ISLAND
Mount de la Touche
HOTSPRING ISLAND
Juan Perez Sound
BURNABY ISLAND
ANTHONY ISLAND *(Ninstints)*
Rose Harbour
KUNGHIT ISLAND

Hecate Strait

MORESBY ISLAND
San Cristoval Range

Queen Charlotte Strait

Port Hardy
Port McNeill

Kyuquot Sound

Strait of Georgia

Campbell River
Mount Washington
Strathcona Provincial Park
Comox
Courtenay

Nootka Sound

FLORES ISLAND

Clayoquot Sound
Tofino
Wickaninnish
Pacific Rim National Park (Long Beach)
Ucluelet
BROKEN ISLANDS
Barkley Sound
Cape Beale Lighthouse
Bamfield
Somerset Range
Tsusiat Falls
Pachena Lighthouse
Carmanah Pacific Provincial Park
Pacific Rim National Park (West Coast Trail)
Carmanah Lighthouse
Port Renfrew

Port Alberni
Mount Arrowsmith
NANAIMO
GULF ISLANDS
Sidney
VICTORIA

Juan de Fuca Strait

VANCOUVER ISLAND

NANAIMO
GABRIOLA
Harmac
DE COURCY GROUP
VALDES
Trincomali Channel
Stuart Channel
Chemainus
GALIANO
Strait of Georgia
Ganges
Active Pass
MAYNE
Crofton
SALTSPRING
PREVOST
Swanson Channel
PENDER
Plumper Sound
SATURNA
Duncan
Fulford Harbour
S. PENDER
Satellite Channel
Saanich Inlet
Swartz Bay
Sidney
SIDNEY I.
D'ARCY
Haro Strait

VICTORIA
Esquimalt
Oak Bay
Sooke

SOUTHERN VANCOUVER ISLAND & THE GULF ISLANDS

Jagged rock and deafening surf on Moresby Island's west coast.

A lazily meandering river flowing into one of Graham Island's many lakes became a fascinating subject.

Many of the aerial images in this book were taken from this Hiller 12E helicopter which is owned and operated by Andrew North of Go Island Hopper Helicopters, Victoria, B.C.

The repeating forms of coastal ridges on Moresby Island are awash in ethereal light as they emerge from a departing storm.

The quality of light after a cleansing rainstorm is particularly treasured by photographers. Here, the partial cloaking of Langara Island by the dispersing storm clouds enhances the magical aura of this remote place.

Three seagulls glide on the air currents over a tidal channel on Graham Island.

Joseph Rocks, north of Hippa Island, provided an excellent opportunity to photograph a sea lion "haul out." In order not to disturb them the pilot spiralled the helicopter slowly downward from a high altitude until the sea lions were in range of the powerful telephoto lens. In the second image, a sea lion has just given birth; the pup is still attached to its blood-red placenta.

Sea caves are not uncommon in the Queen Charlottes. This unusual double sea cave seems to be standing watch over the treacherous rocks.

Large flocks of seagulls circle a small island off the west coast of Graham Island.

Heading north up the west coast of Graham Island, the rock formations begin to take on their own peculiar and distinctive characteristics.

PAGE 23

The rugged west coast of Moresby Island offers some of the most breathtaking images.

PAGE 24

A bald eagle returns to its aerie (nesting site) and its down-covered eaglet. A pair of wings, all that remains of the eagle's last kill, lie in the nest. The bald eagle is a protected species in North America and the Charlottes are home to the greatest number of breeding eagles in Canada.

PAGE 25

A cliff face, typical of the wilder west coast of Graham Island, plummets into the sea. The terrain on Graham Island includes every variation, from dense forest to rocky mountain peaks.

PAGE 26

Poised on a flat tidal ledge off Graham Island's north coast, the majestic column of Pillar Rock (29-metres, 95-feet high) has been an occasional nesting site for Peale's peregrine falcons.

PAGE 27

The *USATS Clarksdale Victory* broke in two off Hippa Island during a fierce winter storm in 1947. Only four of the 53 crew members survived. This aerial viewpoint clearly shows the rusted-out decks and broken rigging of the wreck.

PAGE 28

The steep canyons of the San Christoval Mountains on Moresby Island make for a challenging journey. Extremely punishing turbulence and bone-numbing cold are the norm at that altitude.

PAGE 29

The images of the San Christoval Mountains, taken in late spring, are among the photographer's favourites.

PAGES 30-31

An astonishing range of colours emerges from the mountains on Moresby Island.

PAGES 32-33

The soft evening light draws a startling luminescence from the lush greens blanketing the slopes of the San Christoval Mountains.

PAGES 34-35

Fog sinks into the valleys of the San Christoval Mountains on Moresby Island.

From over Moresby Island, crosshatched with logging roads, and across Skidegate Inlet, Queen Charlotte City appears like a thin line along the shore. Almost the entire population of the Queen Charlottes is settled along the water's edge.

PAGE 36

Carved into a mountainside deep in the San Christovals, the abandoned Tasu Iron Mine looks like the ruins of a lost Aztec temple.

PAGE 37

A massive marine fog bank creeps eastward over Moresby Island.

PAGE 38

A brilliant rainbow dips into the forest on Graham Island.

PAGE 39

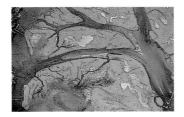

On Graham Island, a river bed at low tide confuses the eye, with logs appearing like toothpicks scattered on a grassy plain.

PAGE 40

A rare and healthy "albino" Golden Spruce stands out on the banks of the Yakoun River in the Queen Charlotte Islands.

PAGE 41

The legendary Haida village of Ninstints is called Skungwai by the Haida. From the air it is easy to see the submerged channels which the Haida cleared in the rocks to more easily and safely draw their canoes up on the beach.

PAGE 42

This unusual view of Ninstents shows totem and some mortuary poles along the shore. The bones of an honoured family member would have been piled into a cavity at the top of the pole.

PAGE 43

Hidden in a quiet cove on Kunghit Island, Rose Harbour was once a bustling whaling station. Early in this century it employed mostly Chinese and Japanese workers. Rose Harbour is now inhabited by a few people who purchased the old station in 1978.

PAGES 44-45

Distinctive rock formations are characteristic of the Queen Charlottes' coastline.

PAGE 46

Hotspring Island in Juan Perez Sound. The hot springs, with temperatures reaching 72° Celsius (162° Fahrenheit), are situated in the rocks near the beach.

A gentle haze follows a storm on Moresby Island.

All that remains of the *Pesuta* is her sun-bleached, weathered bow. The 2,150 ton log barge ran aground in the Queen Charlottes, near Tlell, in 1928.

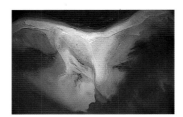

Just off the shore near Sandspit, the fascinating patterns of this shifting tidal bar can only be fully seen from the air.

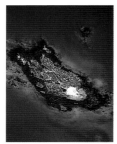

One of the many enchanting and evocatively shaped reefs off the Queen Charlotte Islands.

The radiant hues of twilight linger on in the Queen Charlottes.

Storm clouds gather ominously over Skidegate Inlet in the Queen Charlotte Islands.

Hovering at about 1,200 metres (4,000 feet) above Saturna Island and facing west, the islands of North and South Pender appear to be joined. Beyond North Pender is Saltspring Island and, in the distance, Vancouver Island.

The ferry terminal on Mayne Island, with the fading wake of a ferry in the foreground.

Although few in number, the white sand beaches of Clayoquot Sound on Vancouver Island are often deserted, making them all the more enticing. On the opposite shore the lower portion of the slope is covered with second-growth forest, with old-growth forest above.

Vancouver Island's magnificent and handsomely rugged Pacific Rim National Park encompasses Long Beach, the West Coast Trail, the Broken Islands, and 22,000 hectares of ocean (total area is 51,300 hectares).

PAGE 58

A spring morning looking north along the Pacific Rim and over Pachena Lighthouse, one of 41 lighthouse stations operating in British Columbia. All but five of them are occupied.

PAGE 59

Marking the northern edge of the West Coast Trail, the lighthouse at Cape Beale watches over the infamous Graveyard of the Pacific. A natural stone bridge connects a small rocky island to the main grounds. [118]

PAGES 60-61

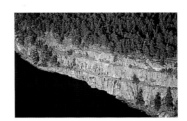

The distinctive markings of a cliff face on one of the Gulf Islands are heightened by the black water.

PAGES 62-63

D'Arcy Island is the haunting site of a former leper colony, in operation from 1891 to 1924. Until 1907 the lepers lived in appalling conditions, receiving supplies only once every three months. Recent visitors have written of feeling overwhelmed by deep sorrow and despair, as though an unseen presence does not want them to leave.

PAGE 64

One of several double-faced waterfalls found in Pacific Rim National Park.

PAGE 65

Hikers from all over the world have been lured to the renowned West Coast Trail to experience the five-day wilderness hike through Pacific Rim National Park. At low tide, a stone arch acts as a natural gateway.

PAGE 66

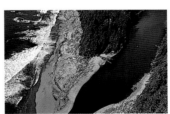

The 77-kilometre (48-mile) West Coast Trail was originally established in the early 1900s to provide a life-saving land route for distressed sailors. The manually operated cable car, one of four along the route, is a rare sign of civilization.

PAGE 67

Pleasure craft bask in the tranquil waters of Pacific Rim National Park, just south of Clayoquot Sound.

PAGE 68

A few of the Broken Islands sparkle like precious emeralds in the deep waters. A favourite destination of kayakers and canoeists, the Broken Islands reward visitors with frequent sightings of killer whales, bald eagles and other abundant wildlife.

PAGE 69

PAGE 70

Looking westward over Clayoquot Sound, Flores Island rests on the distant horizon. The open Pacific appears beyond.

PAGE 71

Wickaninnish Centre on Long Beach provides a look-out for Pacific grey whales on their migration north. As many as 20,000 pass within sight of Vancouver Island on their 10,000-kilometre (6,200-mile) journey—the longest migration of any mammal.

PAGES 72-73

The beacon at Carmanah Lighthouse signals the entrance to the Strait of Juan de Fuca. Government plans to automate 14 more lighthouse stations were abandoned amid protests from coastal communities.

PAGES 74-75

This pastoral setting in the Gulf Islands weaves a serene tapestry into the surrounding landscape.

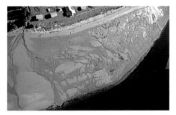

PAGES 76-77

A view of Long Beach in the soft morning light includes several cows strolling lazily home from a deserted stretch of sand at low tide.

PAGE 78

A fiery winter sun sets over southern Vancouver Island, with a communications tower breaking through the cloud.

PAGE 79

The pulp and paper mill at Crofton on Vancouver Island is dramatically back-lit on a crisp, clear winter's evening.

PAGE 80

A small log boom breaks the water's surface into a multitude of patterns.

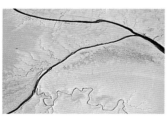

PAGE 81

The ebb tide reveals fascinating textured patterns carved into the mud flats.

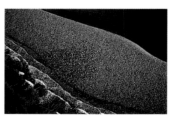

PAGES 82-83

A flock of seagulls enjoys the late evening light on a Vancouver Island sandbar.

Towering nearly 1,800 metres (6,000 feet), Mount Arrowsmith on Vancouver Island reaches gracefully into the skies, as if to bask in the soft, golden light.

Mount Arrowsmith on Vancouver Island.

Red Pillar Mountain stands as one of the crowning jewels of Vancouver Island's stunning Strathcona Provincial Park.

Mount Washington Ski Resort on Vancouver Island looks like a sunlit island in the sky, cradled by the surrounding peaks of Strathcona Provincial Park.

The Mayne Island lighthouse at the entrance to Active Pass is bathed in soft winter light.

A few ferry passengers are intrigued by the aerial intrusion, as the *Queen of Victoria* sails into Swartz Bay terminal on Vancouver Island.

The Gulf Islands attract every type of pleasure craft imaginable. This extravagant yacht, with its own helicopter on the rear deck, was found cruising the waters off Gabriola Island.

The Swiftsure Lightship Classic yacht race is the largest of its type in the Pacific Northwest. This colourful yacht is competing in the 50th Annual Swiftsure (1993).

A competitor in the annual Nanaimo to Vancouver bathtub boat race. Due to their unpredictable and sometimes violent movements, the bathtubbers provide photographers with a great challenge, especially when they must be pursued at low altitudes in a speeding helicopter.

Nanaimo, in the background, is host to the annual bathtub boat race (the 27th race was held in 1993). Many of the 100 or so high-powered bathtubs will sink during their frenzied dash across the open, rough waters of the Strait of Georgia (over 50 kilometres, 109 miles). The fastest race time is 1 hour 19 minutes.

Summer campers take prime spots at the water's edge, in Ruckle Park on Saltspring Island.

An early morning ferry departs Swartz Bay heading into Satellite Channel and through the Gulf Islands. Saltspring Island dominates the horizon on the left.

A golfer's paradise on Gabriola Island.

This lantern house was installed on Trial Island, not far from the mouth of Victoria's inner harbour, in 1908. Three shipwrecks are nearby, including the *Velos* which sank in 1895. The *Velos* had been towing a barge to pick up limestone for the Parliament Buildings in Victoria.

Established in 1893, the 18-hole Victoria Golf Club offers players spectacular ocean and mountain views on a superb seaside links golf course. Here, players take advantage of Victoria's moderate climate, just a few days after New Year's.

This marina on the Saanich Peninsula is home to some of the nearly 8,000 pleasure craft moored in the Victoria region.

A farmer's field on the Saanich Peninsula creates a tableau of agricultural symmetry.

As the sun sets near Crofton on Vancouver Island, patches of snow mark areas of forest that have been clear cut.

A fish-eye lens captures the aerial action above Victoria's inner harbour. Mt. Baker in Washington State glistens on the distant horizon.

The *Alina*, a 130,000-ton Greek freighter, put into port for repairs while en route to Prince Rupert to pick up grain destined for Saudi Arabia.

In the heart of Victoria's old down-town, the quaint shops, restaurants and courtyard of Market Square are popular gathering places.

PAGES 104-105

The mysteries of alchemy are revealed as the copper steeples of St. Andrew's Cathedral (circa 1892) reach above the evening shadows to catch the light that will turn them to gold.

PAGE 106

Government House, the official residence of B.C.'s Lieutenant-Governor, is the fourth residence built on this site. The original structure, erected in 1852, lasted only three months before it was razed by fire. Its two successors suffered the same fate, in 1899 and 1957. Opened in 1959, Government House overlooks the Strait of Juan de Fuca.

PAGE 107

The grand old Empress Hotel is a Victoria landmark, serving over 100,000 afternoon teas each year. Built in 1908 at a cost of $1.6 million, with 483 guest rooms, the Empress has had its share of famous guests including Queen Elizabeth II, the King and Queen of Siam, Rudyard Kipling, Spencer Tracey and John Wayne.

PAGE 108

Craigdarroch Castle was built in Victoria in the 1870s by Robert Dunsmuir, a Scottish immigrant who made his fortune from Vancouver Island coal.

PAGE 109

The Victoria Conference Centre, opened in 1989, has won three architectural design awards.

PAGE 110

A bold abstract of vibrant colours is created by the roof of the Saanich Commonwealth Place in Victoria. The facility, which houses five swimming pools, was built for the 1994 Commonwealth Games.

PAGE 111

Designed in 1872, Victoria's Ross Bay Cemetery overlooks the Strait of Juan de Fuca and the Olympic Mountains. The cemetery, which contains 27,000 graves, is the final resting place for many of Victoria's most prominent former residents.

PAGE 112

No impression of Victoria would be complete without a view of the magnificent Parliament Buildings. The designer was a fledgling architect named Francis M. Rattenbury. Opened in 1898, their cost of $924,000 caused an uproar in the Assembly.

PAGE 113

The inky blue waters of Victoria's inner harbour. Looking north up the Saanich Peninsula, the Gulf Islands appear suspended in the fading light.

PAGE 114

Canada's famous aerobatic demonstration squadron, The Snowbirds, come to Canadian Forces Base Comox each year for spring training. Although they are based in Saskatchewan, many of their aerial sessions are photographed against the breathtaking backdrop of Vancouver Island.

⌁ TECHNICAL INFORMATION ⌁

RAZOR-SHARP FOCUS, ultra-fine detail and optimum colour saturation are Russ Heinl's benchmarks, long before an image is even evaluated for its compositional merits. To maintain these high standards during the aerial sessions, two gyro-stabilized Nikon F4S camera systems were loaded with slow speed film. Auto-focus lenses were used, in configurations ranging from 16 mm fish-eye to 600 mm telephoto lenses. The fine detail and exceptional colour saturation were made possible by Fuji's Velvia™ film, which was used for almost every image in this book. The assignments were flown in a Hiller 12E helicopter or a Hughes 300 helicopter, with the exception of The Snowbirds image, above, which was taken from a Canadair CT-114 Tutor jet trainer.

✠ ACKNOWLEDGEMENTS ✠

Very Special Thanks

to MATTHEW and MEGAN, the two finest children a father could hope to be blessed with. Thank you for your love and unselfish support of all that we do.

to TED GRANT, who inspired me to "see the light" and who gave me the gift of confidence.

to ANDREW NORTH of Go Island Hopper Helicopters in Victoria, who has got to be the finest helicopter pilot ever. I couldn't have done it without him.

to ALLAN MACDOUGALL of Raincoast Books for his long range vision and endless encouragement.

to Beautiful British Columbia Magazine, in particular JOHN THOMSON and BRYAN McGILL.

to THE HONOURABLE ROBERT ROGERS, for his generous support in helping to complete the book in such fine fashion.

to DR. GEORGE MacDONALD, Executive Director of the Canadian Museum of Civilization. His observations and input on the Queen Charlottes have been an invaluable source of inspiration.

to ALEX FISCHER, whose tireless assistance and creative energy have gone such a long way in helping to bring this book to its conclusion.

Thanks also to the British Columbia Ministry of Tourism, in particular BILL SHILVOCK, LARRY LEONARD and JILL JACOBSEN; Pacific Rim National Park; Strathcona Provincial Park; NEIL CAREY, author of *A Guide to the Queen Charlotte Islands*; to fellow photographer, GORDON LEE; STEVE GOOD and GARRY BENNETT of Lens & Shutter, Victoria; ROB TYLER and the gang at Island Transparency Services in Victoria; HENRY and BARBARA at Ken-Lab; GEORGE JANG at CustomColor in Vancouver; MARSHA LEE of Fuji Photo Film Canada for her encouragement and support. To GOETZ, our wild mountain-man guide in the Charlottes; the Gwaii Haanas Management Board; Environment Canada, Parks Service, Queen Charlotte, B.C.; KEVIN NEARY at the Royal British Columbia Museum in Victoria; the Canadian Coast Guard Helicopters; and to The Snowbirds, in particular MAJ. DEAN RAINKIE and CAPT. MIKE LENEHAN, for the greatest flying in the world and the biggest adrenaline rushes I've ever had.

Lastly, my deepest thanks to ROBERT BATEMAN, who so graciously offered his time and lent his meaningful and eloquent words to this book. His encouragement is one of the very special things that has made *Where the Eagle Soars* such a unique and rewarding experience.